Alaska's Little Chief

Traditional Chief David Salmon and the Fur-bearers of Alaska

By
Judy Ferguson

Illustrated by
Nikola Kocić

My name is David Salmon.
Today, I am an Episcopalian priest and the Traditional Chief of Interior Alaska.
I am 95 years old.
Before my birth, when my father was a young man, the great Gold Rush brought
many white men to our land.
At the same time, a bad sickness swept through our people.
After I was born in 1912, the illness reached my family even though we lived far
away where the river is the only road.

When I was little at our home on the Salmon River, near the Black, Porcupine and Yukon Rivers, my father gave me my first little bow and arrow. He said as I grew and proved myself, I would get a bigger arrow made of caribou horn. While I was out hunting one day when I was ten, my mother died of the great sickness. My father said she was going far away by toboggan. He turned to me and said, "You must get away from this sickness. We will leave home and live by trapping. I will teach you how and you will become a man …"

My father put traps, dried fish for us to eat, and caribou hides to keep us warm in our toboggan. He led me to a hill. He quietly placed a new medium-sized bow and arrow into my hands. My father said, "You will climb many hills, and you will shoot your arrow farther than before. God will help you escape this sickness. Then, someday, you will return – and you will help your people." As ravens circled overhead, I drew my bow, and my new arrow flew over the trees, over the hills, and over the rivers where I would travel and learn to become a man.

"Huh! Let's go!" my father called to our sled dogs, Snap, White,
Reiko and Bully. We flew out of the village and into the hills …
with an ermine leading the way.
Startled by our team, suddenly a grouse fluttered out of the brush.
Drawing his big bow back slowly, my father quickly
got our breakfast …
As storm clouds covered the morning sun, my father pointed to a
caribou watching us from a hill.
In the afternoon, he pitched our tent. We piled spruce branches,
caribou hides and down bags inside for our beds. The little ermine
crawled in too!

In the tent, before we slept my father told me and my little ermine the story of Monster Lake. "Before the white men came to Alaska, we always canoed in a lake near here. But stories started," my father said. "Something strange, dark and long was seen in that lake. Moose began to disappear. One fall evening, I saw something in that lake that was long with triangular points on its back. It seemed like it had a mouth, too!" My father added, "Now, we never go to that lake in the summer! We only go when the ice protects us from the creature!" (I was sure my bow and arrow could have taken care of that monster!)

I woke in the morning snug in my warm
duck feather bag on top of my caribou hide
with my little ermine nearby. My father
added a piece of firewood to the crackling
birch bark burning in the Yukon Stove.
Sweet smoke curled up the stovepipe as frost
crystals from the canvas ceiling melted into
my eyes. Delicious smells of boiling grouse
filled my nose. The dogs stirred as a squirrel
chirred. I reached for my bow and arrow.

But it was time to go! We harnessed the dogs to the toboggan and mushed up a hill to set our first traps. (The little ermine was still trailing behind.) Father knelt in the snow to make a "marten cubby," a tiny hut of branches where we set the trap for catching fur. I whispered, "Father, look!" A lynx with its funny, long legs was bounding after a rabbit! My father said I could use my bow and arrow, and that day, I caught our rabbit stew!

In the evening while my father prepared marten hides, he began his nightly stories for
me and my ermine. He remembered a time when he was mushing his team
in No Man's Land just after moonrise when suddenly wolves surrounded
his dogs. He grabbed his rifle; the wolves melted mysteriously into the darkness ...
In our tent, our little candle sputtered. As we began to doze, wolves howled eerily in
the distance. But my bow and arrow were near...

The next morning, we slipped dried fish into our bag for lunch and set out to check our traps. As we mushed, I could smell a stinky fox in the brush!
The chickadees were flying, all excited! Something on the trail had torn up the country!
Our first trap was missing! Around the bend, a creature with a face like a little bear waited. "A wolverine!" my father said, "The trap thief! He could rob all our trap cubbies!" But I thought, "Maybe I could get him with my bow and arrow!"

Two and a half months passed; winter dark softened into spring daylight. My father said it was time that I go to school with my sister at the Fort Yukon mission. To be a man, I must learn not only to trap but I must also learn to read and write.

After he prayed for me that night, my father told me the story of "The Little Boy Who Went to the Moon." He began, "Long ago, a little boy with a bow, who was a friend of the mink, the beaver and the otter …" but with my bow and arrow next to me, I was already fast asleep.

In the spring, as we nudged our boat up to the landing, the mission at Fort Yukon looked so large! With open arms, my sister ran to meet us. Inside the mission, the stove seemed so big compared to our little Yukon Stove! At first I was scared of white people, but Dr. and Mrs. Burke reached out to us. As Mrs. Burke put her arm around me, I watched our father disappear, nosing his boat back into the river.

One September night while we were waiting for dinner, a girl ran downstairs crying, so upset she could not talk …

Suddenly, townspeople burst into the mission screaming, "The mission is on fire!" But the only water was in the river! We made a bucket brigade to the riverbank, trying to save our home. Not even my

In a few months, the townspeople built us a new
home! That winter, in our new school, I learned
to read and write. At night, I dreamed of the
snowy woods, the marten, fox, lynx, otter, ermine,
beaver, mink, caribou, wolf and wolverine. Before
school one morning, I drew pictures on the frosted
window of their tracks and of me with my bow
and arrow.

One winter night, when the Northern Lights were dancing, my father came for my sister and for me. He had a new wife and he had come to take us home to live. I grabbed my bow and arrow and slipped quickly into my caribou hide pants!

My father took us far away from the sickness, away from the mission, the Yukon, Porcupine, Black and Salmon Rivers to No Man's Land – far away to the Grayling River.

Finally, far in the distance, we saw a snug, little cabin. Smoke curled from the stovepipe. A lantern twinkled in the window.

Shyly, we went to meet our new mother. Next to my bed, I put my bow and arrow.

My father turned and faced me, saying, "David, you are ready now
for a sharper arrow. You have aimed high and well. You have been to Fort Yukon;
God has kept you from the sickness. Someday, you will go to faraway places like
Washington, D.C., the nation's capital. You will take care of your
people. Your arrow will go *very* far …"
But that night, I was only eleven. I had traveled far. As my new
mother tucked me in, I slept in my own down bag and I dreamed of my
arrow sailing past the fox, the lynx, the ermine, the beaver, the otter,
the wolverine, the mink, the caribou and the wolf. I dreamed of a
boy growing … into a man …

Glossary

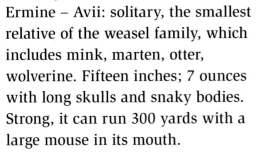

Wolf – Zhoh: wolves range in packs over a 600 square mile area throughout Alaska, about one wolf per 25 square miles. Often gray or black, the adult males weigh up to 115 pounds.

Chickadee – Ch'idzigyak: small songbirds—5 to 5½ inches long, living year-round in the North's forests.

Ermine – Avii: solitary, the smallest relative of the weasel family, which includes mink, marten, otter, wolverine. Fifteen inches; 7 ounces with long skulls and snaky bodies. Strong, it can run 300 yards with a large mouse in its mouth.

Beaver – Tsee: the largest northern rodent, beaver eat bark and plants. Between 1853-1877, Hudson Bay Company sold three million beaver pelts to England.

Wolverine – Nahtryah: a scavenger with large teeth; powerful jaws; dark brown, long dense fur with a creamy white/gold "diamond" stripe. Weighs 20-45 pounds. Solitary; few; travel up to 40 miles a day. It has frost-free fur and is highly valued.

Red Fox – Neegǫǫ: head and body total up to 32 inches; it weighs up to 15 pounds. Fox like hills, valleys and marshes, and are not easy to catch.

Key to Gwich'in words:
ł: a combination of l and s.
k', ch': glottalized consonants. Pronounced with tension in vocal cords finished with a little popping sound.
' (glottal stop): sounds like the pause in the middle of the English word "unh-unh" ("No").
ts, tr and dz: Pronounce as if they were sequences in English words.
Nasal hook (example: ą) : the vowels are pronounced as is usual but with mouth and nose in position to pronounce "n" or "m".

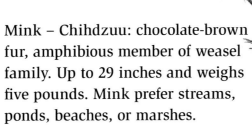

Mink – Chihdzuu: chocolate-brown fur, amphibious member of weasel family. Up to 29 inches and weighs five pounds. Mink prefer streams, ponds, beaches, or marshes.

Marten – Tsuk: soft, dense fur from pale yellow to dark brown; body up to 25 inches; weighs 3 pounds. Usually alone; feeds on mice; member of weasel family; prefers forest. Trappers average 20 to 30 marten a year.

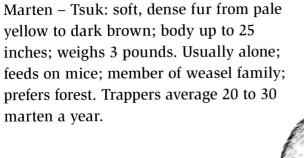

Snowshoe Hare – Geh: up to 20 inches long; 3 to 4 pounds; gray in summer and white in winter, hares cycle from 600 animals per square mile some years to very few in other years. Important food for northern fur-bearers, particularly lynx.

Lynx – Ninjii: weigh up to 30 pounds with an 8-11 year cycle of abundance. Curious animals with long legs, furry feet, a short tail and tufts on each ear.

Spruce Grouse – Treegwat: a game bird called "spruce chicken," are forest dwellers. Have a band of rusty brown on the tip of the tail.

Raven – Deetryą': largest song and all-black bird in the world. Scavenger and predator; an excellent flier; makes 30 distinct calls.

Vowel symbols:
Two vowel symbols together indicate a vowel that takes longer to say.
i, ii: ee, longer ee (like ea in reach, I in machine)
o, oo: o (oa in goat), oo (oe in toe)
e, ee: e as in 'bet', ee like ay in "nay"
u, uu: u as in 'rude', uu like u in 'rule' - more or less.
a, aa: a like u in 'but', aa like a in 'father'

Bow – K'iłt̖a̖į; Arrow – K'ì'; Gwich'in Athabascan nation consists of approximately 9000 indigenous people in Alaska; the Yukon Territory; the Northwest Territories, Canada. Traditionally, young boys used only blunt tipped arrows and short bows. As they grew, their weapons progressed until as teenagers, they received a grown up-sized bow and arrow.

St Stephens Mission, Fort Yukon: Episcopalian hospital and mission dedicated to helping the sick and orphaned during Alaska's tuberculosis epidemics. Located in the largest Athabascan village in the Interior.

Toboggan – Dach̖a̖aval: built closely to the ground with an upturned front bow making it easy to ride over downed trees. Runners were a bed made of 4 5-inch boards connected to the toboggan. The sides were two halves of half-tanned moose hides.

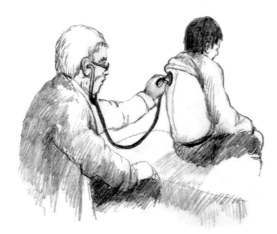

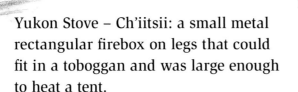

Tuberculosis – a chronic bacterial infection commonly of the lung.

Yukon Stove – Ch'iitsii: a small metal rectangular firebox on legs that could fit in a toboggan and was large enough to heat a tent.

Chalkyitsik (pron: Chell keet' sik) A Gwich'in Athabascan village on the Black River, David's home; latitude: 66.635797; longitude: -143.760465. Population: 83.

In the animal names in the story, stress is on the second syllable of a two-syllable word. Some longer words have two stresses.

"The history of this country is not known. Young people don't know it and old people die with it. I don't want to die with it. I want the young people to have it."
Rev. Chief Dr. David Salmon, Tanana Chiefs Conference First Traditional Chief.

David Salmon, First Traditional Chief, 2004-2007

Andrew Isaac, First Traditional Chief, 1972-1991.

David Salmon and Peter John, First Traditional Chief, 1991-2003.

David teaching tool-making to the young, 2004.

My name is David Salmon. In 2004, I became Tanana Chiefs Conference First Traditional Chief of the Interior's 42 villages.

In 1972, TCC named Chief Andrew Isaac of the Upper Tanana the original First Traditional Chief. When Andrew Isaac died in 1991, Peter John of Minto replaced him as First Traditional Chief. When Peter John died in 2003, I became Chief.

A Gwich'in Athabascan, my mother was from Old Crow country and my father was from near Arctic Village.

My grandfather, King Salmon, was born about 1815, and was nearly eight feet tall. He poled freight boats for the Hudson Bay Company.

When I was a young boy, we pulled one boatload of supplies for the winter, wearing no rubber boots, up the rivers to our cabin. We hunted and fished as we traveled.

Tuberculosis was rampant in those days. Dr. and Mrs. Burke of St. Stephens, the Episcopal mission at Fort Yukon, took care of the sick and orphaned. There was no government assistance.

When my mother died in 1923, I wondered, "Who's going to take care of me...?" I had a little bow and arrow, my only toy. To protect me from the epidemic, my father took me from the village. In the evenings, he told me stories about the migrations of our people. We had no radio and the stories went right to my heart. He told me about Fort Yukon and sometimes, Washington D.C. I never thought I would go any of those places.

That spring when it was time to trade furs, my father decided I was too young to trap, and took me to the mission. I couldn't speak any English but I learned Crackerjacks at the store! (And inside, there was a toy!) I was scared of the horses in Fort Yukon and of the white people. But Mrs. Burke was kind; the kids at the mission followed her like she was a mother duck. Every day, we ate good food and slept in a warm room.

Two years later when my father remarried, he came for me and my sister. He put enough supplies for a year and us into a boat with a heavy inboard. We went far upstream, past Salmon Village and into the Grayling River. After building a base cabin, we mushed deep into the wilderness where we trapped for the next eighteen years. We were the only ones from the Grayling River to the Canadian border: us, the animals and the mountains.

As we trapped, my father taught me how to make and use our traditional tools. In the evenings, while we skinned, my father told me stories of the Hudson Bay Company. When they first arrived, they taught the Natives to jig and play the fiddle. (I missed Fort Yukon's dances and felt like I was in No Man's Land!)

At the mission, I met Sarah. When I was 17, we married. Sarah helped me read and write better. I always tried to learn from other people.

Sarah and I trapped out of the Grayling River but I mushed to get our mail in Salmon Village. When I was 29, I was made chief of Salmon Village. Wanting to get a government-funded school, the people asked me to move from the Salmon to the Black River. In 1941, we began Chalkyitsik village on the Black.

There was no air freight at that time so I began freighting supplies with my boat from Fort Yukon to Chalkyitsik and Arctic Village. I started the Native-run store in both villages and then, I brought logs into Chalkyitsik for a school. I introduced the celebration of potlatch; began dog races and brought the first Christmas tree into our village. We were a happy, little village but we had no church.

I worked construction in Fort Yukon during the 1950s. I began studying the Bible there with Albert Tritt and became converted. When he died, I asked the minister at St Stephens if I could work with the church so they sent me to Michigan to Bible School.

I asked Bishop Gordon in Fairbanks if they would relax the requirements for ordination of the priesthood of four years of college and three years of seminary for Natives.

In 1962, I became the first ordained Native, Episcopal priest in the Interior. Over the years, I traveled from Point Hope to Annette Island and often to the Lower 48. I served as Archdeacon of Interior Alaska and of the Yukon.

In 1962, I went to Tanana for the new Tanana Chiefs Conference and testified regarding the proposed Rampart Dam on the Yukon River. I met Chief Andrew Isaac there and began talking more with Chief Peter John. In the early 1980s, we organized the elders' organization, Denakkanaaga. The old chiefs' words are life to the young.

Today, I share traditional Indian Law and subsistence tool-making with my son, William Salmon, and adopted daughter, Sarah Henry, and grandchildren, Patti, Woodie, Darryl and Willie Salmon, Isabelle Carroll and the adults and children throughout Alaska. In 2002, the University of Alaska honored me with an honorary doctorate of law.

By tradition, Indian Law requires fathers to teach the necessary tools of life to their sons. The scriptures are my tools of life. I tell others when they honor me, they are honoring God Whom I serve. With such tools, our people will survive another thousand years.

Masi Choh Rev. David Salmon

("Masi Choh" Gwich'in "thank you.")

For David Salmon (1912–2007), Janet Curtiss and Alaska's first people; in memory of David Ainley, Christmas 1923-Dec. 30th 2006, Reb, Clint, Heather, Sarah, Ben, Hunter and Halle Ferguson. Judy Fergusc

For the children of the world and for my family: Dušica, Slobodan and Jelena Kocić. Nikola Kocić

<u>*Improved edition. Lesson plans available for all titles:*</u> **Alaska´s Secret Door, Alaska's Little Chief, Alaska's First People, Blue Hills, Parallel Destinies** *and* **Bridges to Statehood.**

Judy Ferguson, freelance columnist Fairbanks Daily News-Miner and Anchorage Daily News. Voice of Alaska Press, formerly Glas Publishing; author of **Parallel Destinies, Blue Hills;** children's books, **Alaska's Secret Door** and **Alaska's First People**. Education: University of Oklahoma; Colorado College; University of California at Los Angeles. Forty–one year resident of Big Delta, Alaska.

We welcome reader response: email: outpost@wildak.net; P.O. Box 130, Delta Jct., Alaska, 99737.
 http://www.alaska-highway.org/delta/outpost/

Illustrator, Nikola Kocić, 5-year graduate of the Fakulte of Applied Arts, Belgrade, Serbia-Montenegro, majoring in Illustration and Graphics under Professor Rastko Cirić, published weekly in the New York Times as well as Professor Gordana Petrović. **Alaska's Secret Door** is Nikola's first book. Email: nkocic1979@yahoo.com; address: Bulevar Nemanjića 76/69, 18 000 Niš, Serbia (Former Yugoslavia.)

Rev. Chief Dr. David Salmon is a master musician, and toolmaker who has made several pre-contact canoes and tools on display at the University of Alaska Fairbanks; the Doyon Corporation Building in Fairbanks; and the Alaska Native Heritage Center in Anchorage. He is the founder/pastor of New Life Ministries. With money from his toolmaking skills, he ministers throughout Alaska and hosts revivals in Chalkyitsik.
http://www.tananachiefs.org/corporate/chief_salmon.html; http://www.episcopalak.org/special_article_message_from_fds.htm

Layout: Sonja Mijajlović, Belgrade, Serbia and Nikola Kocić.
Nikola's paintings were digitized with a Mamiya 16 megapixel by photographer Sonja Mijajlović.
Maps: Nikola Kocić.
Thanks to the staff of Politika and to Publikum Printing.

Credits:
Gwich'in Language: Hishinlai' "Kathy R. Sikorski"; Tom Alton; Siri Tuttle – University of Alaska Fairbanks, Alaska Native Language Center; Katherine Peter; Rev. Chief Dr. David Salmon.

Editors: Marian Sexton; Karen Fraser; Joyce McCombs, Library Director, Delta Community Library; Janet Curtiss; Delta Elementary School, Mrs. Hannah Hudgin's 4th and 5th grade class.

Photos: Judy Ferguson and Nikola Kocić portraits by Sonja Mijajlović, Belgrade, Serbia; Andrew Isaac photo, courtesy of Laura Sanford; David Salmon and Peter John, Denakkanaaga conference, Huslia by Tom Thompson, courtesy of David Salmon; David Salmon photos, courtesy of Janet Curtiss and David Salmon.

Second paperback edition: January 2007.
Library of Congress Cataloguing-in-Publication Data.
Printed in Belgrade, Serbia, Publikum Printing.
Text and illustrations© 2007. Judy Ferguson
Third paperback edition, January 2009.
ISBN 978-0-9716044